The Nature Kid's Guide to
SNOWY OWLS

DAVID ANDERSON

LP Media Inc. Publishing
Text copyright © 2026 by LP Media Inc.
All rights reserved.

For information address LP Media Inc. Publishing,
30012 Variolite St NW, Princeton MN 55371
www.lpmedia.org

Publication Data

Snowy Owls
The Nature Kid's Guide to Snowy Owls — First edition.

Summary: "Learn all about Snowy Owls, the Nature Kid Way"
— Provided by publisher.

ISBN: 979-8-89818-151-2

[1. Snowy Owls – Non-Fiction] I. Title.

Title: The Nature Kid's Guide to Snowy Owls

CONTENTS

Frozen Fields 4

Northern Nomads 6

Big Birds 8

Fluffy Feathers 10

Super Senses 12

Snow Camo 14

Lemming Lunch 16

Silent Swoop 18

Watch Out 20

Fight Back 22

Glide Low 24

Day Shift 26

Solo Hunters 28

Sky Dance 30

Cute Chicks 32

Devoted Dads 34

Warming World 36

Helping Hands 38

FROZEN FIELDS

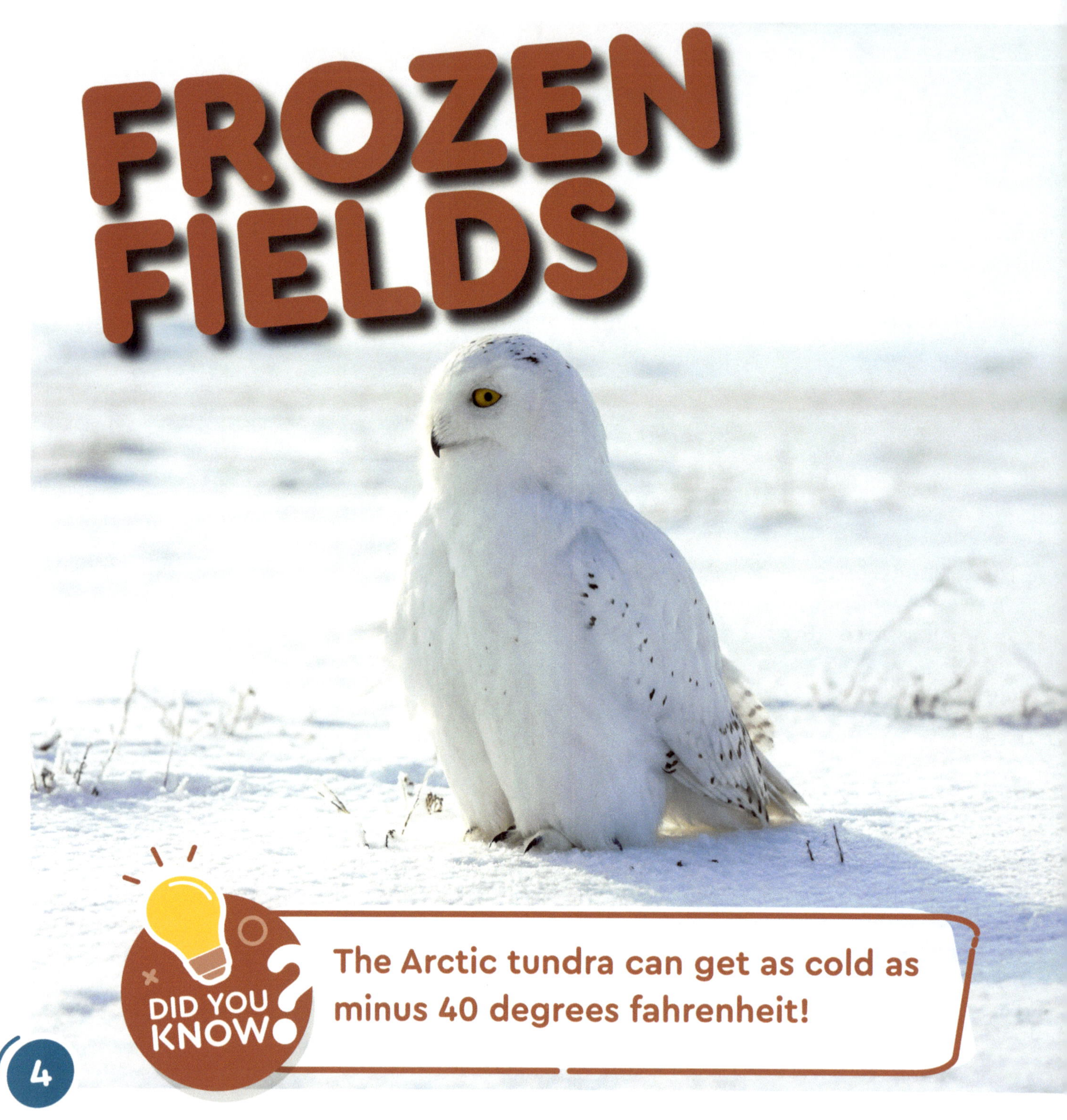

The Arctic tundra can get as cold as minus 40 degrees fahrenheit!

Hoot! A snowy owl sits on frozen ground. Its yellow eyes scan the icy land.

Snowy owls live in the Arctic tundra. This is one of the coldest places on Earth. The ground stays frozen for most of the year. Trees do not grow in the Arctic tundra.

The tundra is flat and open. Strong winds blow across the land. Snow covers everything in winter. But summers are short and bright.

Snowy owls like these wide open spaces. They perch on rocks and small hills. From there, they can see all around them. The frozen fields are their home.

NORTHERN NOMADS

Whoosh! A snowy owl soars over the frozen north. White wings cut the air.

Snowy owls live most of their lives in the far north of our planet. They can be found in places like Alaska, Canada, Russia, and Greenland.

These owls are great travelers. In winter, some fly south. These journeys can cover over 2,000 miles!

Snowy owls like to live in the cold north, but will go where food is. If lemmings are hard to find, they move to a new place looking for food.

Snowy owls have been spotted in many U. S. states. They even reached Hawaii once!

BIG BIRDS

Thump! A snowy owl lands on a fence post. This big bird looks for prey.

Snowy owls are large birds. They stand about 2 feet tall. That is as tall as an average dog!

Females are bigger than males. A female can weigh up to 6 pounds. Males weigh a bit less, around 4 pounds.

Snowy owls also have wide wings. Their wingspan can reach 5 feet! This helps them glide over the tundra.

Snowy owls are the heaviest owls in North America. Their thick feathers add extra weight.

FLUFFY FEATHERS

Baby snowy owls have gray, fluffy down. They grow white feathers as they age.

Fluff! A snowy owl puffs up its feathers. It looks like a soft snowball.

Snowy owls have a very thick coat of feathers. These feathers cover their whole body. Even their feet have feathers!

The feathers trap warm air close to the skin. This keeps the owl warm in freezing cold. Snowy owls can stay warm even at 40 degrees below zero.

Each feather has tiny branches called barbs. These barbs lock together like a zipper. This makes a smooth, tight coat. Wind and snow cannot get through.

SUPER SENSES

Screech! A snowy owl turns its head. It heard a tiny sound.

Snowy owls have amazing hearing. Their ears are hidden under their feathers. One ear is actually higher than the other!

This helps them pinpoint sounds. They can even hear a mouse moving under the snow!

Their eyes are sharp too. They can spot prey from half a mile away. They can also turn their heads 270 degrees to look all around.

Snowy owls have eye tubes, not eyeballs! They cannot roll, so they must move their head to look around.

SNOW CAMO

Squint! A snowy owl blends into white snow. This makes it very hard to see.

Snowy owls have white feathers. This helps them hide in snow, so predators cannot spot them easily.

Male snowy owls are almost pure white. Females have dark brown bars on their feathers. Both colors blend in with snowy ground.

Young owls have more dark marks. As they grow older, they get whiter. This camouflage keeps them safe from danger.

Snowy owls have feathers covering their feet and toes. They look like they are wearing fluffy white slippers!

LEMMING LUNCH

Gulp! A snowy owl catches a Lemming. It's time to eat!

Snowy owls eat mostly lemmings. These small rodents live in the Arctic. One owl can eat up to 1,600 lemmings in a year!

Snowy owls also catch other prey. They hunt voles, rabbits, and birds. Sometimes they catch fish or ducks near water.

These owls swallow small prey whole. They cannot chew their food. Later, they cough up bones and fur in a **pellet**.

Scientists study owl pellets to learn what owls eat.

SILENT SWOOP

FUN FACT!

Snowy owls catch prey hidden under snow. They punch through with powerful feet!

Swoosh! A snowy owl dives from the sky. Its wings make no sound.

Snowy owls are silent hunters. Their feathers have soft edges. This muffles the sound of flapping wings.

They watch from a perch or the ground. When they spot prey, they swoop down fast. Their attack comes without warning.

Snowy owls grab prey with sharp **talons**. Their feet are strong enough to catch animals while flying low over the ground.

Sometimes they hover in the air, waiting for the perfect moment. Then they drop straight down on their target.

WATCH OUT

Growl! A red fox creeps closer. The snowy owl watches it.

Snowy owls face few **predators**. Their large size keeps most hunters away, but some animals still try to catch them.

Arctic foxes hunt owl eggs and chicks. Wolves will attack nests too. Adult owls must guard their young carefully.

Golden eagles are a threat to adult owls. These big eagles can catch a snowy owl on ground or even while it is in flight!

Sometimes snowy owls pretend to be hurt to lead predators away from nests!

FIGHT BACK

Screech! A snowy owl spreads its wings wide. It hisses at a fox.

Snowy owls can fight back. They use sharp talons and beaks to hurt attackers.

Parent owls dive at threats from high in the air. They swoop down from behind so the predator does not see them coming. They strike with their sharp talons and fly back up before the predator can react. They will attack again and again until the threat leaves.

Snowy owls are so fierce that they will chase away foxes, wolves, and even bears.

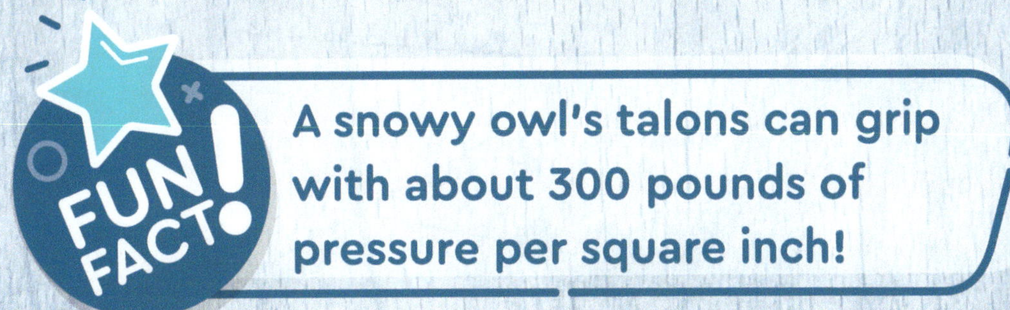

GLIDE LOW

Swoop! A snowy owl glides above the grass. Its golden eyes scan for prey.

Snowy owls fly low to the ground. They stay close to the earth when hunting. This helps them spot small animals hiding below.

They can fly up to 50 miles per hour. Strong wings carry them across open land.

Snowy owls can also walk and even run on the ground. They will chase their prey through grass and snow.

Snowy owls can travel over 1,500 miles in one winter. They may visit the same spots each year.

DAY SHIFT

Squint! A snowy owl blinks in bright sunlight. It is wide awake.

Most owls hunt at night. But snowy owls are different. They hunt during the day.

This makes sense for where they live. In the Arctic summer, the sun never sets. It stays light for months at a time.

Snowy owls rest on rocks or small hills. They watch for prey in the daylight. Their eyes work well in both bright sun and dim light.

In winter, snowy owls may hunt at dawn and dusk. They adjust to shorter Arctic days as sunlight fades.

SOLO HUNTERS

Crunch! A snowy owl sits alone on the snow. No other owls are near.

Snowy owls live alone most of the time. They do not form flocks like some birds.

Each owl hunts by itself. It does not share its hunting ground with others.

Snowy owls only come together to mate. After chicks grow up, the family splits apart and each owl goes its own way.

Snowy owls know their neighbors by voice. They can tell one owl's call from another!

SKY DANCE

Squawk! A male snowy owl takes off, he is about to perform his sky dance!

Male snowy owls perform sky dances each spring. They fly up high, then swoop down in waves.

The male also carries food during his flight. This shows the female he can hunt well.

After mating, the female lays eggs on the ground. She makes a shallow nest called a scrape. There are very few trees in the arctic, so they must make ground nests.

A female snowy owl can lay up to 16 eggs in one nest. She lays more when food is plentiful.

CUTE CHICKS

DID YOU KNOW?
Snowy owl chicks call to their parents from inside the egg! They make sounds two days before hatching.

Chirp! Fluffy white chicks huddle together, waiting for food.

Snowy owl chicks are born with their eyes closed. After about five days, their eyes open. Baby owls have white down at first.

Eggs hatch about two days apart, so the oldest chick hatches first. A nest can have up to 11 chicks!

Chicks triple their weight in the first week. They will eat about two lemmings each day!

Until their own feathers come in they stay warm by huddling under their mothers feathers.

They can fly when they are about 50 days old.

DEVOTED DADS

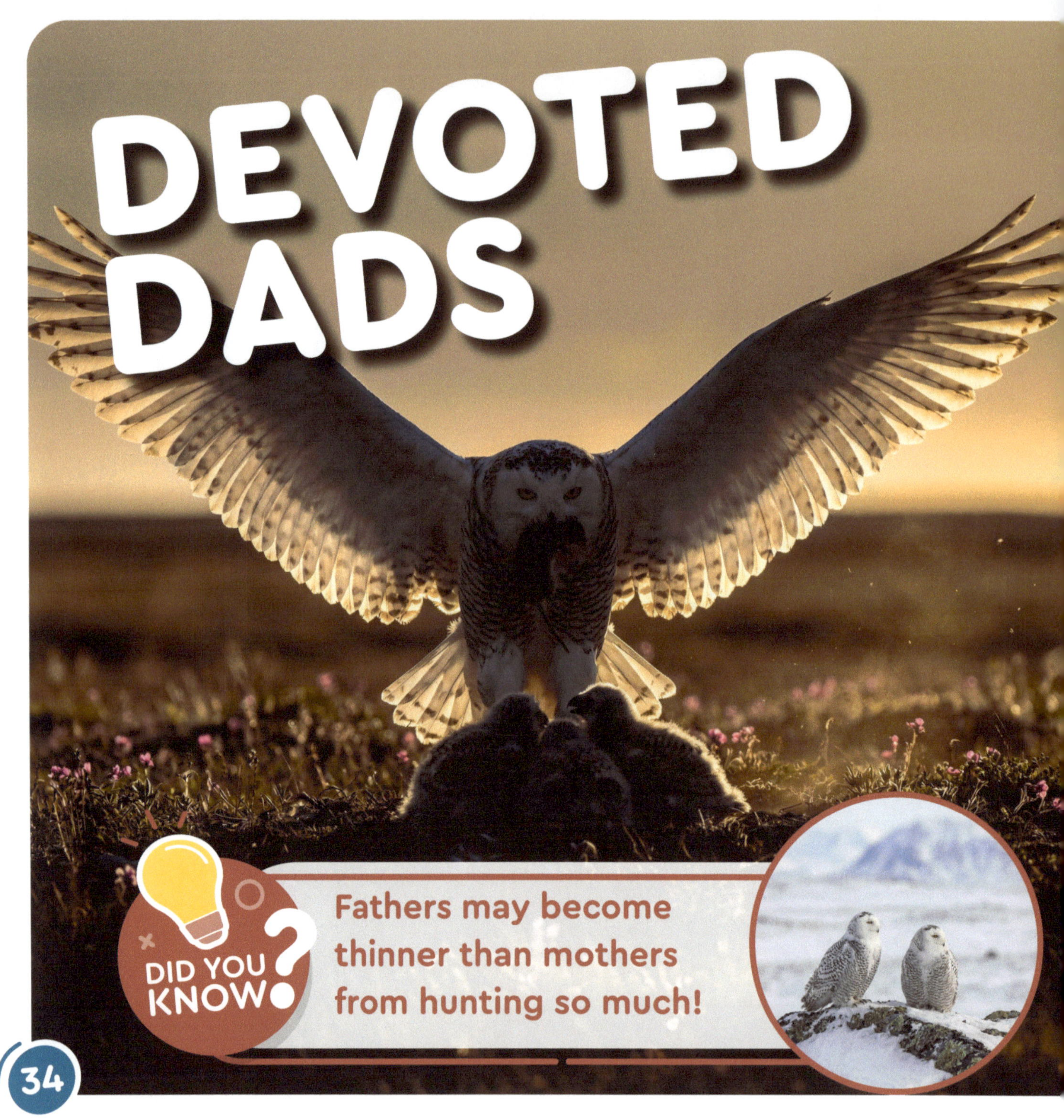

Stomp! A male snowy owl lands with a lemming in his beak.

Male snowy owls help raise their chicks. The father brings food to the nest many times each day.

The mother stays with the eggs and chicks to keep them warm. This means the father does all the hunting during this time.

Fathers also guard the nest. They chase away animals that come too close. A father may attack foxes or even wolves to protect his family.

Both parents work hard for about two months. Then the chicks can hunt on their own.

WARMING WORLD

Crack! Arctic ice breaks apart. A snowy owl searches for solid ground.

Earth is getting warmer. This is a big problem for snowy owls.

Warmer weather melts Arctic ice and snow. Snowy owls nest on the ground in the open tundra, so these changes affect their homes.

When the Arctic warms, lemming numbers drop. Fewer lemmings mean less food for owls.

The Arctic warms four times faster than the rest of Earth. This also threatens polar bears, seals, and walruses.

38

Buzz! Scientists attach a small ID tag to an owl's leg.

People work hard to help snowy owls. Scientists track where owls fly, which helps them learn what owls need.

Some airports have special teams. They safely move owls away from runways. This keeps both owls and planes safe.

Groups also protect owl nesting areas. They teach people how to watch owls without scaring them. Everyone can help snowy owls!

Some airports use trained dogs to find snowy owls hiding in grass and move them to safety.

GLOSSARY

tundra
A very cold, flat land where no trees grow.

camouflage
Colors or patterns that help an animal hide.

talons
Sharp claws that birds use to grab things.

pellet
A small ball of bones and fur that an owl spits up after eating.

predators
Animals that hunt and eat other animals.